Shelter in Place

poems by

Rob Hardy

Finishing Line Press
Georgetown, Kentucky

Shelter in Place

Copyright © 2022 by Rob Hardy
ISBN 978-1-64662-767-7 First Edition
All rights reserved under International and Pan-American Copyright Conventions. No part of this book may be reproduced in any manner whatsoever without written permission from the publisher, except in the case of brief quotations embodied in critical articles and reviews.

ACKNOWLEDGMENTS

Third Wednesday: "Letter," "Icicles," "Floodplain Forest," "Wild Onion"
Willows Wept Review: "Shelter in Place," "Coda"
Lost Lake Folk Opera: "Variations," "Grounded," "Light"
Poems from the Lockdown, ed. Trevor Maynard (Willowdown Books 2020): "Crossing the Delaware"
Undocumented: Great Lakes Poets Laureate on Social Justice, ed. Ron Riekki and Andrea Scarpino (Michigan State University Press 2019): "My Mother's Pussy Hat"
19th Annual Poet-Artist Collaboration (Red Wing Arts): "The Stump"
20th Annual Poet-Artist Collaboration (Red Wing Arts): "Flood Plain Forest," "Prairie Tale"
End in Mind Pandemic Poetry Project: "Variations," "Shelter in Place"

Publisher: Leah Huete de Maines
Editor: Christen Kincaid
Cover Art: Matthew Klooster
Author Photo: Clara Shaw Hardy
Cover Design: Elizabeth Maines McCleavy

Order online: www.finishinglinepress.com
also available on amazon.com

Author inquiries and mail orders:
Finishing Line Press
PO Box 1626
Georgetown, Kentucky 40324
USA

Table of Contents

[This month's moon] 1

Letter 2

Icicles 3

My Mother's Pussy Hat 4

Shelter in Place 5

Closure 6

Variations 7

Crossing the Delaware 8

Coda 9

Lyrical Dresses 10

Two Poems for Jane Kenyon 11

Reopening 12

Today's Headlines 13

The Great Conversation 14

Floodplain Forest 15

The Stump 16

Prairie Tale 17

Grounded 18

Wild Onion 19

Closing Time 20

Light 21

In memory of Miriam Hardy
1936-2021

This month's moon

This month's moon
shines in the sterile distance,
nothing touching its face but light.

Letter

In those days, we wrote letters.
We licked a stamp
and placed it in the corner of the envelope.
The stamp cost 13 cents.
I still have a letter you wrote me
the day after a snowstorm almost fifty years ago.
I can still see you making a path
through the snow to the birdfeeder,
the scribble of sunflower seed on the ground.
As you sat at your desk
you could watch the birds through the window—
chickadees, juncos, purple finches.
In the spring, you wrote, the ground
would be littered with the empty husks of seeds.
You have been dead for thirty years,
but there in the ink is the shadow of your hand,
and sealed behind the stamp,
your tongue.

Icicles

We live inside a cave of ice.
We look out ice-barred windows ablaze
with frozen sunlight
and watch them form,
the icicles,
sharpened to the melting point,
tapering to liquid flame,
candle's
polar opposite,
like some Pleistocene
calendar-clock
lengthening with the days,
seasonglass
slowly
spill
ing
in
to
s
p
r
i
n
g

My Mother's Pussy Hat

On Monday, an ice storm postponed
the Martin Luther King celebration.
Ice coated the streets and the sidewalks.
There was no firm footing anywhere.
Overnight, the rain turned to snow
and the world went suddenly white.
On Tuesday morning, I cleared the ice
from the sidewalk in front of the house,
because this is how we do things
in a cold climate: we give ourselves hernias
so that others won't break their necks.
A sidewalk reminds me that the borders
of our lives are porous, that to tend
our own small frontage on democracy
we must take on the burden of strangers
and put our backs into the work.
I spent the whole week wondering how.
On Friday afternoon, a dense fog rose,
too much like the ghost of something
we had left to die. In spite of the darkness
and unsteady hands, my eighty-year old mother
stayed up all night knitting herself a hat. All night
it grew from its long umbilicus of yarn,
taking the shape of something
both pantherine and gynecological.
When Saturday dawned, pink and hopeful,
my mother's pussy hat was one
of millions, as if with enough pink yarn
women could knit a whole nation back together.

Shelter in Place

Of brown and gray there is no end.
It is enough to be silent
in the presence of such silence.
The chorus of frogs has not yet
bubbled to the surface of the marsh,
but the milkweed pods open like mouths
and spill their eloquence. In the rain
my body makes the same music
as the prairie grass. We share
the same pulse, the same quieter breathing.

Closure

Last night,
after thirty-five years of dreaming
I couldn't remember
the combination
of my college mailroom box,
I finally remembered.
At the same time, I knew
the mail inside
would be for someone else.

Variations

Corvid: a type of bird, crow or raven,
an absence of light perched
ominously on the bare branch
of a roadside tree,
descending after the impact
to dance.

*Ovid: a poet who wrote We are slow
to believe in the things that cause us harm
and Abundance has made me poor.*

Comorbid: existing simultaneously
in a patient. As in, anxiety and depression
are frequently comorbid. As in all
the comorbidities of March:
sap running and ice going out,
the song of the red-winged blackbird
and the color brown,
chapped hands and empty shelves.

Covid-19: at this distance from yesterday
and one another, sometimes
we have to be the bird
singing somewhere in the woods, who for now
exists only as its song.

Crossing the Delaware

I.

George Washington,
where have you been?
Slipped from the ATM
in more innocent times
(three weeks ago),
flimsy token of communicable value,
six minutes of labor
at the current minimum wage,
but currently unemployed,
possible disease vector
quarantined in my black billfold.

II.

A virus almost ended the country before it began. In 1776, smallpox raged through the Continental Army, more fatal to the cause than Redcoat muskets, killing three of every ten.

The public feared inoculation, which was the best defense against the pox, and Congress banned it.

Washington, watching the decimation of his troops, recommended quarantine and inoculation. It had never been done before, inoculation on such a scale, an entire army herded into immunity.

III.

Washington was famous
for his strategic retreats.
To cross the Delaware
was to buy more time,
to wait things out,
to flatten the curve.
To prevail,
sometimes we have to disappear.

Coda

This winter took all the repeats.
April felt like a recapitulation of March,
a leitmotif of snow running through the forecast,
sometimes the deceptive cadence
of a seventy degree day.
In April, we listened to robins
singing in the wake of the storm,
a fugue of chromatic juncos,
and we waited for spring to make its entrance,
for the last measure of snow,
the first note of green in the trees,
buds blaring open like trombones
in the fourth movement of a Brahms symphony.
It seemed like spring would never come,
and then it came. Winter's white tune
is taken up by the wild plum,
and the trees have changed
their key from gray to golden-green.
The snow has taught us not to say
this is the end, but on a day
like today we know we've begun
the season's brief modulation into summer.

Lyrical Dresses

For Daphne and Joy

I knead bread to indulge my sense of touch.
I take long walks to breathe deeply.
Often I stop to look at the trees.
The glow and fade of trees
as clouds move across the sun.
Trees dancing to the choreography of wind.
This morning I looked up "lyrical dresses"
to learn what the maples are wearing
as they sway outside my window.
Sometimes I feel like I'm looking at ordinary life
through the wrong end of a telescope.
Everything close to me seems so far away.
Sometimes I cry for no reason.
Sometimes I sing because I feel the urge to sing.
It's like this every day.

Two Poems for Jane Kenyon

i.

I read a poem to start the day,
like a vitamin, a small dose of dailiness.

You open a drawer or stand in a doorway,
and there is light, but no startling epiphany—
only the quiet persistence of things.

And it stays with me throughout the morning,
the feeling that you have given me
your eyes, each poem a small bequest of light.

Four buzzards kettle over the marsh, one crow
like an asterisk in the margin of their flight.
They fling their shadows out over the prairie,
motes in the eye of the sun. Suddenly gone.

ii.

The snail lives inside its burden.
The cat sings to its enemy, the door.
In the pause between thunder,
the loudest thing is the voice of the wren.

Reopening

The leaves come in their own time.
The maples are winded and summer-green
before the oaks and cottonwoods commit.
In other years, so much of this
happened without my noticing. Today,
in the woods above the marsh,
fragments of sunlight and turbulent shadow:
the shadow of a red-tailed hawk, multiplied
by aspen and birch, moves swiftly up the trees.
I feel it, too, as if I have become something much smaller.
I want to stay like this a while longer.

Today's Headlines

Crows perform a caw and response outside the window.
Squirrels have moved in above the kitchen ceiling.
The owls nesting in the cottonwood have had their owlets.
Rice County has the highest rate of new cases in the country.
Showy orchids are blooming in the woods.
The squirrels chew holes in the eaves and dig holes under the porch.
The state recently purchased an abandoned warehouse for the dead.
Lilacs are blooming a month earlier than a century ago.
States are easing restrictions even as new cases continue to rise.
Each time we fill a hole, a new hole appears.

The Great Conversation

In isolation, I find myself
talking, not to myself,
but to the world around me.
I ask the flower's tight-lipped bud
what it will be when it blooms.
I compliment the catbird on its song
and speak reassuringly to the sparrow
who hops ahead of me on the path.
I speak to the trees, who speak
to each other underground but answer me
only with the whisper of leaves.
Still I am part of a great conversation.
I ask a question of the kestrel
treading air above the prairie burn.
For all the answer it gives me,
I might as well be talking to God.

Floodplain Forest

The wind in the cottonwoods
sounds like rain before the rain,
as if from growing beside the river
they have learned its language,
translating the sound of water
into leaves and air. The roots
push into silt, the branches
reach to the silt-colored sky.
The river, when it widens and slows,
becomes a mirror, a transcription
of cottonwoods and clouds.
At the top of a cottonwood, herons
rise in waves from raft-like nests
on wings the color of silt and sky.
Wind squalls through the leaves.
The woods are drenched in sound.

The Stump

It fell in a late September storm
before its leaves had a chance to turn,
a sugar maple laid across one lane of traffic
in a tangle of shattered green.
After the storm, chainsaws came
and swarmed around the wreck,
filled the air with sawdust and racket,
left nothing behind but a stump.
It's hard to let go of absence.
It's what remains. In the spring,
the roots felt warmth on phantom limbs,
and from the blind earth
drew sap to fill the memory of buds.
The stump was glazed
with a maple's sticky sweet hereafter.
One last time it blossomed
as the butterflies came to drink,
orange wings like the resurrection
of autumn leaves, wind-shaken
and suddenly falling upward.

Prairie Tale

for Nancy Braker

I find her kneeling in the prairie
like a seed just shrugging off the earth.
I half expect her to photosynthesize,
turning green as she rises toward the sun.
She tells me she's attempting to propagate
a plant called bastard toadflax.
All around, there is magic—
the grass spinning itself into gold,
purple wands of liatris conjuring butterflies,
compass plants enchanted by the sun.
The midsummer prairie is a cauldron of green.

Grounded

> *Is our world gone? We say "Farewell."*
> *Is a new world coming? We welcome it.*
> *—Lyndon B. Johnson (quoted on pages 20-21*
> *of the U.S. passport)*

My new passport has never been anywhere.
It lies in an old shoebox,
like a dead pet awaiting burial,
with unspent euros and European plug adaptors,
maps of Athens and central London
and other places we visited in a different world.
The box says New Balance.
Sometimes I take out my expired passport
and look at the stamps—
London, Frankfurt, Osaka, Athens—
remembering how I stood in line
to receive them like a sacrament,
remembering the places themselves, the pieces
of myself left there, irretrievable.
The future feels like unclaimed baggage.
There's nowhere else in the world I can go.
I'm thinking of getting a better box.

Wild Onion

for Jessica Morrison

I like the nodding wild onion,
its umbel of blossoms like fireworks,
a pastel constellation unseasonably pink
among the purples and goldenrod of August.
Its color and beauty are its own.
To see it for the first time was to witness creation,
to welcome some miracle into the world.
Whenever I see its pink halo in the grass,
I pause to give it my attention,
as if its existence were a call to prayer—
praise for its bright crown,
praise for its hidden onioniness
and its small globe of tears underground.

Closing Time

We sit on the deck of the Fairfield Inn,
our first evening out in six months. Despite
his mask, I recognize one of the waiters
from last summer, and it reassures me
to see he's still alive. I order the same
cocktail as last time. A heron appears
over the river, half an hour darker than dusk.
The young people upwind at the end of the deck
are laughing, but at our table the conversation
hovers like flies around something rotten.
The last time we sat here, we were planning
a trip together, a wedding, projecting
ourselves painlessly into the future.
This feels like the end of the world
instead of the end of another Thursday.
The sky exhales its darkness.
Everything casts a shadow,
then becomes shadow.
None of us wants another round.

Light

Through the sleepless night Orion
still strode above the rooftops of the town.
The sunrise still unfurled its pink and blue
as if announcing a birth. The sun still rose,
and as it rose it burnished the prairie grass.
Nothing had been taken from the beauty of the world.
Even the raucous geese were beautiful
with the light of morning on their wings.
Even the gray November woods were filled with light.
A young woman stepped from the path
to walk in the fallen leaves,
just for the pleasure of the music they made.
She smiled, and the leaves whispered at her feet.
The light seemed to rise up from the earth,
up the stems of the grass, into the bare branches of the trees.
The light was all around us. And still it rises.

In addition to *Shelter in Place*, **Rob Hardy** is the author of the full-length collection *Domestication* (2017) and the chapbook *The Collecting Jar*, which won the 2005 Grayson Books Poetry Chapbook Competition. His writing, both poetry and prose, has appeared in *Rattle, New England Review, Ploughshares, West Branch, Best of the Net,* the anthology *33 Minnesota Poets* (2000), and numerous other journals and anthologies. His poems also appear on sidewalks in Northfield, Minnesota, and on the walls of the Northfield Public Library and Prairie Creek Community School.

Rob Hardy holds a Ph.D. in Classics from Brown University. As a classicist, he has produced a commentary on selections from Bede's *Historia Ecclesiastica* (Dickinson College Commentaries) and translated two Greek tragedies for performance at Carleton College, where he is a research associate and occasional visiting assistant professor in Classics. For most of the 1990s, he was a stay-at-home father to his two sons. He has also been a K-12 substitute teacher and an elected member of the school board, and received a public service award for his work as an advisor to the Northfield Skateboard Coalition.

In 2016, Hardy was selected as the first Poet Laureate of Northfield, Minnesota. As Poet Laureate, he has hosted monthly poetry readings by local and visiting poets; taught poetry workshops for children, seniors, and developmentally-disabled adults; received two regional arts council grants; judged the state Poetry Out Loud finals; and written and read poems for numerous public events in Northfield.

Many of the poems in *Shelter in Place* are inspired by the poet's daily walks in the Carleton College Cowling Arboretum during the pandemic year of 2020.

www.ingramcontent.com/pod-product-compliance
Lightning Source LLC
LaVergne TN
LVHW041522070426
835507LV00012B/1758